STAR GAZING

Contemplate the Cosmos to Find Inner Peace

By Swapna Krishna

Cover Art by Kyutae Lee
Interior Illustrations by Liana Jegers

POCKET NATURE

STAR GAZING

CHRONICLE BOOKS

SAN FRANCISCO

POCKET NATURE SERIES

Text copyright © 2023 by **SWAPNA KRISHNA**.

Library of Congress Cataloging-in-Publication Data available.

ISBN 978-1-7972-2136-6

Manufactured in China.

Series concept and editing by **CLAIRE GILHULY**.
Series design by **LIZZIE VAUGHAN**.
Cover art by **KYUTAE LEE**.
Interior illustrations by **LIANA JEGERS**.

Typeset in Albra, Benton Sans, Caslon.

10 9 8 7 6 5 4 3 2 1

Chronicle books and gifts are available at special quantity discounts to corporations, professional associations, literacy programs, and other organizations. For details and discount information, please contact our premiums department at corporatesales@chroniclebooks.com or at 1-800-759-0190.

Chronicle Books LLC
680 Second Street
San Francisco, California 94107
www.chroniclebooks.com

CONTENTS

But I know,
somehow,
that only when
it is <u>DARK</u> enough,
can you <u>SEE THE STARS</u>.

—Martin Luther King, Jr., "I've Been to the Mountaintop"

W hen you think about the night sky, it's easy to feel small. After all, the universe seems infinite. There are more stars in the sky than grains of sand on a beach. That kind of scale is so big, it is incomprehensible—the human mind can't grasp how huge the universe is. To make matters even more complicated, the cosmos is actually expanding at an accelerating rate. There are new stars being born every day. It's easy to feel lost.

But the night sky can also be a welcoming place. At first glance, it might appear cold and distant, but then you remember that each one of those stars is burning brightly. There's warmth there. Stars can remind us that we do have a place in the universe, and that it's okay to shine. That each of us matters. Regardless of where you are on this planet, even if you're far from home in a place you don't recognize, the night sky can provide something familiar.

I've been looking at the stars ever since I was a child. Curiosity about what was out there led me to my current profession as a science journalist and a space writer. And throughout my life, I've been trying (and often failing) to be a "good" meditator. Meditation is in my religion, my heritage, and my blood, and yet, for most of my life, I always felt inadequate when I tried to meditate. It took me a long time—too long, really—to understand that there isn't a right or wrong way to do it. You can't "win" at meditation. It just is. When you let go of expectations, meditation becomes comforting. A retreat from the world.

Stargazing can also be a form of meditation: a comfort, a source of mystery, a wondrous and awe-filled experience, familiar yet entirely foreign. People have been looking to the night sky for the entirety of human history; cave paintings from prehistoric times depict the night sky and crude constellations connecting the stars. Curiosity about the sky around us, starting even before we understood its nature or that there were other planets, has been a fundamental part of human existence.

Many ancient civilizations connected their religious and cultural belief systems with the stars. There are currently eighty-eight official constellations recognized by the International Astronomical Union (IAU), an organization that promotes and supports astronomy. Over half were identified by the ancient Greeks, while the planets are named after ancient Roman gods (well, all except for our own planet). This doesn't mean that stargazing was exclusive to these cultures, though. Every civilization has its own stories about the stars.

While the North American and European understanding of astronomical history is rooted in these ancient Western cultures, people around the world have endeavored to make sense of the night sky. Ancient Chinese astronomy focused on accurate timekeeping

and tracking the days, months, and years,
while Mayans used the stars (specifically the
Sun) for their calendar. Medieval Islamic
astronomy improved upon the Greeks' understanding of the cosmos while Europe was in
the Dark Ages. The Māori new year is timed
to the appearance of the Pleiades star cluster
in the Southern Hemisphere, while ancestors
of the Khoikhoi, traditionally nomadic people
who live in southern Africa, saw the Pleiades
as the end to the rainy season. Many Hindus,
like myself, still view the movement of the
stars as an integral component of our religion.

These days, we know a lot more about the
night sky than ancient humans did, but that
doesn't take away any of the wonder. At their
most basic, stars are luminous balls made pri-
marily of hydrogen and helium, held together
by their own gravity. During their long lives,
they produce elements thanks to the process
of nuclear fusion (in the heat and pressure of
a stellar core, stars fuse hydrogen into helium
and other elements). They burn and burn until
there's nothing left; then, depending on their

mass, they might become stellar remnants, white dwarfs, or even black holes. During this dramatic process of stellar collapse and death, they form heavier elements, such as precious metals. Nearly all of the elements in the universe come from stars. We are all, essentially, made of stardust.

Whether you tie your religious belief system to what we see in the stars or not, looking for constellations and patterns remains a profound and wondrous experience. Connecting with the night sky is a practice in understanding more about who we are and our role in the universe, and in becoming more aware of ourselves and the world around us. Contemplating the night sky is an easy starting point for moving toward a more mindful existence.

Stargazing can be a very personal experience. The stars mean something different to each of us. Maybe you look at them every night. Or perhaps you haven't given them a whole lot of thought. And that's okay. They're there for you whether you think about them or not.

In this book, you'll find a roadmap to the stars. You'll learn the basics about the night sky and all that it holds—from stars to planets and even human-made objects like the International Space Station. There's plenty of science here, but also contemplation of the cultures and rituals of stargazing around the world (and not just from ancient Greece and Rome, which is so centric in Western culture), as well as meditations that remind us of the power of the cosmos. In the final chapter, you'll find a guide to seventeen constellations visible from the Northern Hemisphere to encourage you to start your own stargazing practice.

When stargazing, the most important thing to remember is that your focus should not be on what you can't find or can't see. Even if you can spot only the moon, you're doing great. The point of stargazing, for our purposes, is simply to look up at the night sky and reflect on the wonder of our world and the universe beyond. The rest will come, in time.

I felt like I had a right
to be ANYWHERE IN THIS UNIVERSE,
that I belonged here
as much as any SPECK OF
STARDUST, any COMET,
any PLANET.

—**Mae Jemison,** *the first Black woman in space, after her flight*

I.

A HISTORY OF STARGAZING

As long as humans have been on this planet, people have been looking up to the stars, wondering what might be out there. Prehistoric cave paintings at sites across Turkey, Spain, Germany, and France show us that ancient humans studied the stars. Even forty thousand years ago, people had a sophisticated understanding of astronomy, chronicling comet impacts and using the stars to track the months and years.

Most of the legends around stargazing that are ever-present in US and European culture (including the official names of many constellations) derive from ancient Greek and Roman mythology, but of course the stars didn't belong to these cultures exclusively. Around the world, every civilization has traditions of stargazing, and understanding how different cultures across history have used it is important.

When considering a civilization's relationship to stargazing, we should ask: Was stargazing a beloved pastime, or was it an integral part of their culture and stories? Did they depict stars simply for artistic reasons or for more practical reasons—perhaps to keep track of time and understand the changing seasons? Stargazing is a vital part of many civilizations, even today. Many Indigenous cultures are still in the process of rediscovering their astronomical roots after colonization, the introduction of new diseases, and resettlement eroded their traditions, practices, and beliefs.

INDIGENOUS PEOPLES OF THE AMERICAS

Stargazing has served many practical purposes for the Indigenous peoples of North America, though many of these traditions have been eroded or lost completely due to contact with destructive European colonizers. Among the Lakota, a people who live on the Plains and who may have originated in the Great Lakes region of what is now the United States, watching the night sky was how they knew when to start planting their crops and harvesting their fields. The Cree, a Canadian First Nations people, credit the stars for teaching them about the Sweat Lodge, an important ceremony of health, purification, and healing.

For the Skidi Band of the Pawnee people, a group originally from the Nebraska area of the United States, the stars were a fully integrated part of their culture and way of life. Tales told by the Skidi Pawnee say their origins were tied to the stars. According to these stories, Mars and Venus, as seen in the night sky, were the parents of the first human girl, while the Sun and moon birthed the first male child.

The Skidi Pawnee even used the stars to determine how they structured their community: Their elders sat in a circle based on circular constellations—like the Corona Borealis—to lead and make decisions for the rest of their people. This gathering was called the Council of Chiefs. They saw their Chief Star, also known as Polaris or the North Star, as a representation of their main god. By replicating what they saw in the night sky on land, the Skidi Pawnee linked themselves to their origin stories, creation myths, and gods in order to embody legitimacy and authority in their governing decisions. Perhaps you can imagine what it must have been like, being a child among these people, believing that you originated in the stars. And in many ways, it's true—we are all made of the dust of stars.

In South America, the Inca and Quechua were remarkable at astronomy and actually wove it into the fabric of their cities. The Sun Gate in Machu Picchu was constructed to mark the solstice, while the layout of Cuzco is modeled on the shapes of their constellations. What's really extraordinary is how they interpreted the night sky. They saw the glowing band of the Milky Way as a river that gave them life, and the dark spaces between the stars as animals that drank from the glowing river in the cosmos, obscuring its light.

PEOPLES OF AFRICA

Ancient humans around the world examined the night sky and participated in some form of astronomy. Monuments like Stonehenge, in England, are testaments to the importance of the night sky within these cultures. In fact, there are plenty of these kinds of ancient celestial monuments across the world—they're just not as well known.

One example is Nabta Playa, located in present-day southern Egypt, which may be the world's oldest astronomical site. It's the site of megalithic structures dating from around 5500 to 3400 BCE (making it older than Stonehenge). Scientists have determined that these particular giant stone structures were likely aligned with Arcturus or Sirius, the brightest stars in the night sky of that period.

Many Indigenous peoples of Africa still value stargazing. The Dogon are an ethnic group from Mali in West Africa who possessed advanced astronomical knowledge before technology caught up and confirmed it.

For example, the Dogon have long believed the planets orbit the Sun, Earth rotates on its axis, and Saturn has rings. Their four calendars follow the Sun, moon, Venus, and Sirius, a star that they worshipped for thousands of years. They have long believed that Sirius has a heavy companion made of metal; the discovery of a second star in the Sirius system in 1862, Sirius B, (an extremely dense white dwarf), showed this belief to be scientifically accurate.

Dogon mythology tells that the Nommos, ancestral spirits, gifted them with this advanced astronomical knowledge. Later, European explorers questioned whether the Dogon people were visited by, or perhaps even descended from, extraterrestrial beings from Sirius.

Among various groups in Nigeria, long-held beliefs and practices around stargazing are ubiquitous, even as the country's experience with modern astronomy is evolving. The Ibo people, the country's largest ethnic group, still live according to a lunar calendar within their own communities. Priests use the motions of the night sky—the moon, planets, and stars—to derive the calendar, which determines market days, seasonal festivals, and other big holidays each year.

THE MĀORI

In the Southern Hemisphere, the Māori people of New Zealand had a rich tradition of astronomy, which is in the process of being rediscovered thanks to organizations like the Society of Māori Astronomy Research and Traditions (SMART). Historically, the Māori relied on their deep understanding of the stars in order to traverse the Pacific Ocean. It's easy to close your eyes and imagine the

ANCESTORS MEDITATION

If you're feeling lonely, try this meditation.
You can do this at any location you can
see the night sky, whether in a city or the
wilderness, even if it's cloudy outside.

It's easy to feel lost and alone in the world.
Sometimes it can feel like everyone else is
busy enjoying their lives, while you're stuck.

When you feel that way, head outside at night
and close your eyes. Allow yourself to adjust to
the darkness. Look up.

It doesn't matter what you can or can't see.
Focus on any celestial object, whether it's the
moon or a star that's calling out to you. If you
can't see anything, imagine a star in the sky,
breaking through the clouds. Think about
that object. Ponder the fact that hundreds or

even thousands of years ago, someone likely looked upon that very object and had the same thoughts you do. Let the stars connect you to your ancestors. What would you tell them about your life? How would they marvel at what you see and do each day?

We can feel lonely, but the night sky ensures we are never truly alone. We always have those who came before us and those who will come after us. Let the night embrace you, and take whatever comfort you can from it.

immense sense of loneliness—but also of wonder—late at night in the vast watery expanses, with only the brightness of the stars to point your way.

Stargazing is woven into the very fabric of Māori culture. Because much of Māori tradition has been passed down orally, their knowledge of the stars has been woven into their customs and language. For example, Venus being close to the moon is considered an ill omen, while the star Antares is mentioned in a proverb advising people to stick close to people of good standing. The Pleiades—or Matariki, as they are called by the Māori—rise in midwinter, and this signifies the beginning of the Māori new year. It's a time when the Māori remember those who have passed and release their spirits to the stars.

The people of Tonga, a Polynesian country in the Pacific Ocean, also traveled the oceans thanks to their advanced understanding of the stars. In fact, stargazing and studying the night sky were treated as a branch of navigation, rather than a science in and of itself.

For many Pacific Islander cultures, gazing upon and understanding the mechanics and movements of the stars, as well as the patterns across them, was crucial to their nautical way of life.

PEOPLES OF ASIA AND THE MIDDLE EAST

In China, the tradition of stargazing and documenting the night sky is age-old. The ancient Chinese record of the night sky was the most accurate (even more so than the records of the Greeks and Romans) until the rise of Islamic astronomy. Much like we do today, Chinese astronomers carved up the sky into regions, which translate roughly to enclosures, symbols, and mansions.

The three enclosures center on the North Star and circumpolar constellations. They then divided the plane on which our planets orbit into four symbols (Azure Dragon, Black Tortoise, White Tiger, and Vermilion Bird); each symbol contains seven mansions, or hsiu, for a total of 28 lunar mansions (also called houses). These follow the path of the moon in the sky, which was important to the ancient Chinese who used a lunar calendar.

Advances from the ancient Islamic world have also been crucial to our modern understanding of astronomy. During the sixth century CE, while Europe was in the Dark Ages, astronomers in the Middle East were continuing to study the night sky. Astronomy was an important part of their religion—after all, precise astronomical calculations helped determine when to have daily prayer and which direction to face for it.

But Islamic scholars were also moved by secular concerns—they wanted to understand the precise operation and structure of the universe. They were the most advanced stargazers from the eighth to the fifteenth century CE, and they influenced civilizations across the world.

THE DARK-SKY MOVEMENT

The night sky is incredibly powerful, and you can see it from anywhere on the planet. But because of light pollution, the sky we see today is very different from the one our ancestors saw hundreds and thousands of years ago.

The International Dark-Sky Association views a dark night sky as "a shared global heritage"—one that everyone should have access to. They advocate for mitigating the impact of outdoor lighting: designing and implementing responsible outdoor lighting that limits unnecessary light, utilizes warmer color tones, and limits brightness levels. It's not feasible to eliminate light pollution altogether—populated areas need to be lit at night. But we can certainly take steps to lessen the impact of outdoor lighting on our view of the night sky.

If you've only ever seen the night sky from a city or urban area, it's worth looking into whether there are any dark-sky preserves near you. While you can observe and meditate upon the night sky from anywhere, the experience of seeing what the sky looks like, of observing the milky band of stars crossing the night sky and understanding the scale of our galaxy, is worth pursuing.

A quick internet search will reveal dark-sky preserves in your area. You can also visit www.darksky.org for a database of international dark-sky preserves, though it should be noted that their listings heavily favor locations in the United States, Canada, and western Europe.

Dark-sky preserves exist in exactly the places you think they would—within national parks and the wilderness—but efforts are also being made to create dark-sky areas accessible from urban areas. Palos Preserves is just 24 miles [39 km] from downtown Chicago, while Valle de Oro is 7 miles [11 km] from Albuquerque, New Mexico. These urban sites are few and far between, but as awareness about stargazing and light pollution grows, they will become more popular, and perhaps more cities will carve out these kinds of nearby preserves.

When you look AT THE STARS AND THE GALAXY, you feel that you are not just from any particular PIECE OF LAND but from the SOLAR SYSTEM.

—**Kalpana Chawla**, *astronaut, after her first flight*

II.

UNDERSTANDING THE NIGHT SKY

The night sky may seem simple—an inky black backdrop with countless white specks dotted across it—but it's actually anything but. It's a place of simultaneous chaos and serenity. To contemplate it is to try and understand it, while also knowing that the human brain is incapable of comprehending the scale of the universe.

When gazing at the night sky as a practice in mindfulness, it might be helpful to understand what you're looking at. Picturing each object as it exists in space can be relaxing and a way to focus your thoughts.

So what can we see when we look up at the sky with the unaided eye? The short answer is planets, stars, the moon, nebulae, and galaxies. The long answer, though, is that it depends.

There are constants within the night sky, to be sure, but it also changes—from season to season, from night to night. What we can see in the sky depends on where we are in the world, the time of year, and what phase the moon is in.

This chapter will equip you with some basic knowledge so that the next time you stargaze, you can start to recognize what you're looking at.

TOOLS TO STARGAZE WITH

All you really need to look at the stars is yourself and a night sky. You don't need to stress out about the right equipment.

If you *do* want to gather some tools, though, what you need is pretty simple. If you're keen on identifying objects when you're

stargazing, there are some great phone apps that can help. Many smartphone apps use augmented reality (AR) technology that allows you to point at a spot in the night sky and label what you see. Just make sure that, when you're using your phone outside, the display is set to be as dim as possible. If you have any features that shift the display to red tones rather than blue, toggle those as well.

Want to leave your technology behind? That's a great practice. Books (like this one!) can help you stargaze. If you're taking books with you at night, consider buying a red flashlight. The color red will preserve your night vision so you can examine any book or text you need to and still be able to make out the details of the night sky.

While binoculars or a basic telescope can open up the night sky and give you a new perspective on stargazing, they aren't necessary. For the purposes of this book, the only tool you'll need is your eyes (and any glasses or contact lenses you might wear for distance vision, of course!).

WHY IS THE NIGHT SKY BLACK?

Let's start with the most basic aspect of the night sky: the sky itself. During the day, it's brilliant blue (or gray, if the clouds get in the way). But at night, it turns the darkest color. That's because of the rotation of the Earth. During the day, the side of the Earth you're on faces the Sun. At night, it faces away, and without daylight obscuring the universe, we can see the wonders of space.

If you live near a city, you may not experience a truly dark night sky. Don't stress out about it. Meditative stargazing is about focusing on what you *can* see, not worrying about what you can't. You can do this as effectively from the roof of an urban building as you can from a dark-sky location in a national park. While it's absolutely worth venturing out to take in truly dark skies at some point, especially for telescope viewing or astronomical events such as meteor showers, it's not necessary for day-to-day meditative stargazing.

The night sky is black because in between each star and planet and nebula and galaxy, there's a lot of empty space. There's so much star stuff out there—but even more emptiness. And every second of every day, that emptiness increases as the universe expands. That's why space is black, and that's why our night sky is as well.

SO WHAT'S OUT THERE AND WHY?

The amazing thing about the night sky is that it's constant and yet ever changing. What you see in the evening isn't going to be the same as your pre-dawn views, even if you're sitting in the same spot. Some constellations appear only during certain times of the year. Astronomical events are often predictable—the annual Perseid meteor shower, for example—but some are surprises, like an asteroid or a supernova. And we haven't even talked about the moon, the most reliable and visible night-sky object, which is completely dark once a month.

Of course, if you travel, the night sky changes based on where you are. The Southern Cross is visible only in the Southern Hemisphere. If you're in the polar regions during the summer, you may not get a night sky at all—just twilight as the Sun dips below the horizon.

But generally speaking, anytime you look at the night sky, you can see a few key things with the unaided eye.

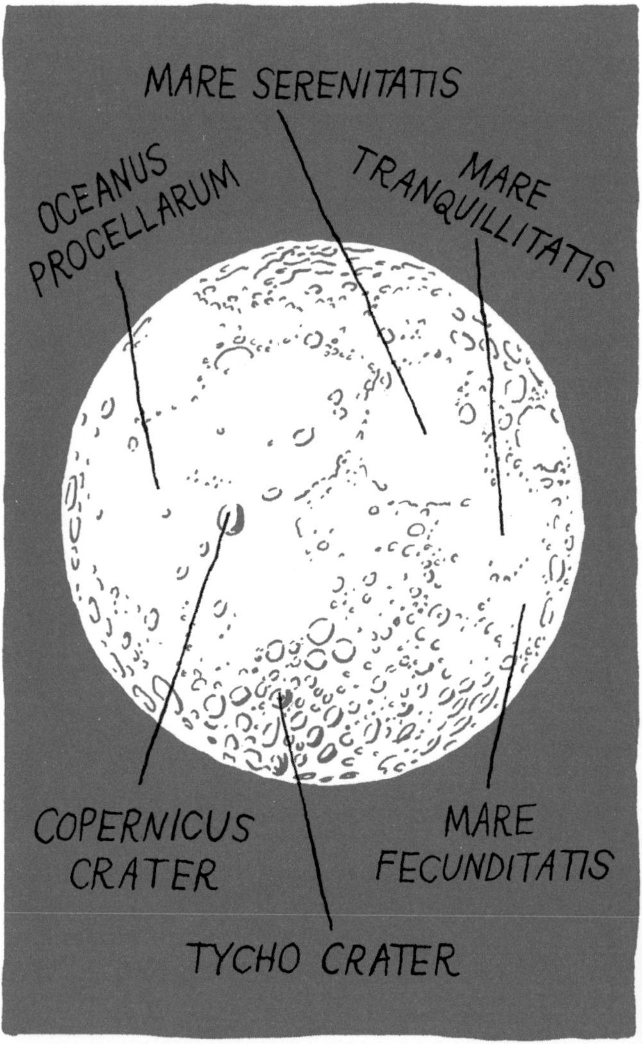
MARE SERENITATIS
OCEANUS PROCELLARUM
MARE TRANQUILLITATIS
COPERNICUS CRATER
MARE FECUNDITATIS
TYCHO CRATER

THE MOON

The moon is the most familiar object in the night sky. Our largest natural satellite is tidally locked to the Earth, which means its orbital period around our planet matches its rotation speed. The result is that we only ever see one side of the moon from the Earth—that's why people refer to the "dark side" of the moon. (In reality, the far side is just as illuminated as the one we can see.)

Thanks to the moon's reflection of sunlight, the moon goes through phases. Each cycle lasts 29.5 days from new moon to new moon. Phases aren't a byproduct of the moon passing through the Earth's shadow (that's a lunar eclipse). Instead, they're our perception of the half of the moon's surface that's illuminated. When there's a new moon, (i.e., the phase when we can't see the moon in the sky), the far side of the moon is what's reflecting the Sun's light.

The solar system formed about 4.6 billion years ago, but the moon didn't come into existence until about a hundred million years later. We still aren't quite sure how the moon formed, but we *do* know that it's almost a twin to the Earth in terms of composition. Moon rocks are similar to Earth rocks, it turns out.

The distance to our moon varies based on where it is in its orbit, but on average it's about 238,855 miles from us (or thirty Earths away). To put that into perspective, the International Space Station, which is in low Earth orbit, is about 250 miles overhead. It's hard to comprehend just how big "outer space" is.

Given that distance, it's incredible what you can see when you look up at the moon without a telescope. The next time you're outside on a clear, dark night, close your eyes. Let them adjust to the darkness around you, and then after a few minutes, gaze up at the moon. Study it. Here's what you're seeing.

At first glance, the dark areas in contrast to the lighter ones are striking. These dark areas are the lunar "seas," or maria (singular: mare), and they cover about one third of the moon's visible surface as seen from the Earth. If you look at the top center of the moon and then move your eyes a little down and right, that is Mare Serenitatis, or the Sea of Serenity. On the southwest side of Mare Serenitatis is a small bright area with a dark spot in the middle—that's the foot of Mons Huygens, the moon's tallest mountain, which is about 18,000 feet [5,500 m] high.

Just to the southeast of Mare Serenitatis is another dark sea. This one is called Mare Tranquillitatis, or the Sea of Tranquility. That is the spot where humans first stood—the landing site of Apollo 11. The sea to the southeast of Mare Tranquillitatis is Mare Fecunditatis, or the Sea of Fertility, which approaches the moon's terminator line, or the line between light and dark.

Move your gaze back to the center of the moon, and then track south from there. You may be able to make out a bright spot in the southeastern quadrant about three-fourths of the way down the moon's surface. That's an impact crater called Tycho. It's actually quite small for how visible it is, just 53 miles [85 km] in diameter. The reason it's so prominent is because it's relatively new—perhaps just one hundred million years old, compared to the one-billion-year age of most craters on the moon. That means its features are more defined now, but eventually age will wear them away.

Now, move your gaze again up and left to another bright impact crater, just above the Northern Hemisphere line. This time, you might actually be able to make out the edges of that crater—it's Copernicus. To the south-west of that is another dark area, Oceanus Procellarum, or the Ocean of Storms.

The moon is lovely to contemplate, and it's amazing what details and features you can see even with the naked eye. A bright full moon can obscure the rest of the stars in the sky, but it's important to focus on what's present rather than what's hidden. When the moon isn't visible or is in its crescent stages is when the rest of the sky comes alive. Darkness shows us the wonder of what's really out there.

MOON MEDITATION

This meditation is good for anxiety or stress on any night there's a moon with visible features. It doesn't have to be a full moon! Don't stress about what you can't see.

Allow your eyes to adjust to the darkness, then look up at the moon. Move your gaze across the maria of the moon's surface, resting on each dark feature. For each one, think about something that makes you anxious or uncomfortable. Hold it close, and then move on to the next one.

Once you've moved across the moon's surface and have named all those fears, zoom out— from the moon and from that anxiety. Look at the moon as a whole. Observe the way the dark and the light meld to form something beautiful. Close your eyes and imagine the moon's imperfect surface, pockmarked with craters. Imperfect is still whole. Imperfect is still beautiful. The imperfect moon still shines and so can we.

Take a deep breath, and let go of those fears. Accept the anxieties. Live in the discomfort. It's okay. Embrace those parts of yourself, because they are you, and that makes them good.

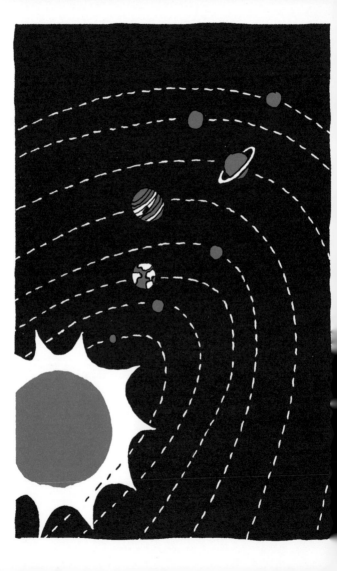

THE PLANETS

Billions of years ago, our solar system was just a cloud of gas and dust. That cloud, called a solar nebula, collapsed, and the Sun formed. The leftover material formed the eight planets—the four inner rocky planets (Mercury, Venus, Earth, and Mars), two gas giants (Jupiter and Saturn), and two ice giants (Uranus and Neptune), and the asteroid belt between the two groups.

It's pretty incredible that we can see some of the planets in our solar system without a telescope. Depending on the time of year and time of night, it's possible to see Mercury, Venus, Mars, Jupiter, and Saturn with the unaided eye.

The most visible planet (and second brightest object in the night sky, after the moon) is Venus. It's bright white, thanks to the Sun's light reflecting off the clouds that shroud the surface from view. Sometimes it's the evening star, meaning it's visible just after sunset. This is when the planet is farthest from the Sun. As it progresses in its orbit, it moves between the Earth and the Sun (this happens every 584 days). It then reappears as the morning star, observable before the Sun rises for the day.

It's hard to say when a planet will be visible (both in terms of time of year but also time of night), because it depends on the position of that planet relative to the Earth and the Sun. The other planets in our solar system have different orbital periods around the Sun and therefore different year lengths; that means they aren't at the same place in our sky at any given time from year to year.

Generally speaking, all the planets you can see appear along the ecliptic, which is the plane of the Earth's orbit around the Sun (see page 54). Occasionally, if everything lines up just right, you can see Mercury, Venus, Mars, Jupiter, and Saturn all at once.

THE ECLIPTIC

The ecliptic is the path the Sun travels across the Earth's sky over the course of a year as a result of the Earth orbiting the Sun. More broadly, it's the plane of the Earth's orbit around the Sun as well as the plane of the solar system.

Most of the planets in the solar system orbit within 3 degrees of the same plane (the outlier is Mercury, which is at 7 degrees). That means that, in our own sky, they are found on the ecliptic as well—that's where you should look, should you be seeking them out any night.

Why do all the planets orbit along the same plane? Space is three-dimensional; shouldn't they be scattered every which way? The answer is, apparently, no—and we've found that the example of our solar system, with the planets lying along a single plane, is replicated across the other star-planet systems we've found in the galaxy.

Scientists think this is because of the way solar systems form, out of a disk of gas and dust surrounding a star. The plane of the planets mirrors the shape of that original disk.

In ancient times, the ecliptic was crucial for navigation because it was one of the few distinct imaginary lines across the sky. That's why the constellations of the zodiac were developed over two thousand years ago—these are the markers of the ecliptic within our sky. The ecliptic runs directly along the center of the constellations of the zodiac. (It's important to note that, while the signs of the zodiac are associated with astrology, astrology is not a science.)

The moon has an important connection to the ecliptic as well. Its orbit does not lie along this plane; it's inclined about 5 degrees off the ecliptic. But solar and lunar eclipses can occur only when the moon's orbit intersects the ecliptic, which is why they're relatively rare.

THE INTERNATIONAL
SPACE STATION

The International Space Station (ISS) has been continuously inhabited since November 2, 2000. That means that every human alive in the universe is not located on Earth. Of course, we've been going to space for decades, but on disparate missions— continuous habitation of a space station has brought an entirely new dimension to humanity's exploration of the stars.

Eventually the ISS will no longer be in orbit. Sometime in the future, probably 2030 or later, it will fall back to Earth in a controlled reentry, burning up in the atmosphere. What's left will strategically crash into the Pacific Ocean, lost to the depths of the frigid waters. (Or maybe not—there are movements to preserve the ISS as an orbital museum.)

But for now, it is in the sky, and you can actually see it passing overhead with the unaided eye if the time is right. It's just a quickly moving light, like an airplane—you can't see its form or structure—but it's visible enough that it will attract your notice even if you aren't looking for it. It's the third-brightest object in the night sky, after the moon and Venus, after all, and most visible in the early morning or evening, in the hours after the Sun has risen or set. If you *do* want to deliberately find the ISS, NASA's Spot the Station website can help (Spotthestation.nasa.gov/).

While other human-made satellites are certainly visible with the naked eye, they're much harder to identify and track than the ISS.

GALAXIES, NEBULAE, AND CLUSTERS

If the night is clear and you're in an area with dark sky, then you may be able to see something extraordinary: a band of stars and light across the middle of the night sky. Believe it or not, that's the Milky Way, our galaxy.

Our solar system is located along the inner edge of the Milky Way's spiral arms. We're about 26,000 light years from the center of our galaxy, which you can't see because of dust and gas, but it's located within the constellation Sagittarius. (The supermassive black hole at the center of the Milky Way is called Sagittarius A*. Learn more about Sagittarius on page 99.)

Our galaxy is staggeringly large—scientists estimate that it's around 120,000 light years across (though it may be even larger than that). There are anywhere from one hundred million to four hundred million stars within it. When we look up into the night sky and see that ghostly band of stars, dust, and other matter (which is just one of the arms of the Milky Way), we're only seeing around five thousand stars at any given time with the unaided eye. And that's when conditions are pretty much perfect for viewing.

The best time of year to see the Milky Way in the Northern Hemisphere is in the summer, when there's a new moon.

The Milky Way is in what's known as our *Local Group*, a cluster of galaxies about 10 million light years in diameter. It's not clear how many galaxies are in the Local Group, but it's reported to be anywhere from thirty to fifty—perhaps even more than that. But we can't see most of them from Earth. The Milky Way galaxy and the Andromeda galaxy (also known as Messier 31 or M31) are the largest galaxies in the Local Group, but there are many smaller galaxies as well. The

Andromeda galaxy is a spiral galaxy located about 2.5 million light years away, and you can see it with the unaided eye in the fall and winter months (see page 106).

Nebulae are clouds of gas and dust in the space between stars, housed within galaxies. They are stellar nurseries, where stars are born. Nebulae are more visibly abundant in our sky than galaxies. The best way to take in these fuzzy objects is to look at the dark sky around them, rather than precisely at them.

The most well-known nebula is the Orion Nebula, located within the constellation of the same name. That's also the location of the Horsehead Nebula. The Eagle Nebula is on the border of what's visible to the unaided eye, but it's worth mentioning because it's the location of the iconic Pillars of Creation, jaw-dropping formations of gas and dust that have been visited and revisited in photos snapped by space telescopes.

Star clusters are large groups of stars that you can see without too much effort. Perhaps the most famous is the Pleiades, which influenced ancient civilizations across the world. But there are quite a few more you can find with some effort, such as the Double Cluster, Alpha Persei, and Orion's head.

You can use constellations to easily find these clusters, nebulae, and galaxies, and we'll talk about that more in the next chapter.

THE STARS

B y far, the most common sight in the night sky is the array of stars dotting its vast landscape. Stars come in all sizes and colors, and they're inconceivably dense objects, but they're also much like us in the ways that matter: They're born, they live, and then they die.

Stars are birthed within clouds of dust known as *nebulae* (some of which—like the Orion Nebula—you can see with the unaided eye!). These clouds of dust and gas collapse because of gravitational pull and become protostars. It takes about fifty million years for these dense, hot protostars to become actual stars.

All stars are long lived (think billions of years), but the lifespan of a star depends mainly on its mass: the more massive the star, the shorter its life. Stars, if they're big enough, fuse hydrogen into helium within their dense cores. This reaction produces an energy that emanates outward. When that outward energy is equal to the star's own gravitational pull inward, the star stabilizes and becomes a main-sequence star, like our Sun.

When main-sequence stars run out of hydrogen, they collapse. For some stars, this brings on the red giant phase. The collapsed core heats up, which fuses the hydrogen remaining in the outer layers, and the star expands violently and burns brightly red.

When a star like our Sun runs out of helium, it becomes a white dwarf. This is the incredibly dense core of a star that loses its luminosity as it cools down.

For more massive stars, the process of fusion at the core continues with elements like carbon and oxygen. This creates some of the heavier natural elements within our universe. These stars continue to fuse elements at their cores until they begin to produce iron. At that point, the star can no longer support its own weight and the entire thing collapses in a huge, fiery explosion called a supernova, which releases an extraordinary amount of energy.

Smaller supernovas result in dense neutron stars, while larger ones become black holes. From the dust and gas left over after a star's death, new stars are born.

· · ·

Types of Stars

There are so many different kinds of stars in the universe. Most of the stars we can see with the naked eye are type B, A, or F stars and red giants. Here's a breakdown of the different kinds of main-sequence stars (stars that are in the adult parts of their lives), arranged from hottest to coolest. An example is listed for each type.

O-TYPE STARS (BLUE GIANTS)

These stars burn so hot that they appear bluish white. Their temperatures range from 25,000 to 50,000 K. (K, or kelvin, is a temperature scale that has no negative values. Absolute zero is 0 K, which is about −460 degrees Fahrenheit [−273 degrees Celsius].) O-type stars live for around forty million years but are comparatively rare.

VISIBLE IN THE NIGHT SKY · ALNITAK

B-TYPE STARS

Also hot and blue, B-type stars range from 10,000 to 25,000 K. They're short lived and, along with O-type stars, are massive enough to end their lives as supernovas and black holes.

VISIBLE IN THE NIGHT SKY · RIGEL

A-TYPE STARS

These white stars are in a temperature range of 7,500 to 10,000 K. They're typically young, but they can live for up to around a billion years.

VISIBLE IN THE NIGHT SKY · SIRIUS
(THE BRIGHTEST STAR IN THE NIGHT SKY)

F-TYPE STARS (YELLOW-WHITE DWARFS)

These white stars are larger and hotter than our Sun, burning at around 6,000 to 7,500 K, and can live up to five billion years.

VISIBLE IN THE NIGHT SKY · PROCYON

G-TYPE STARS (YELLOW DWARFS)

These stars range in temperature from 5,000 to 6,000 K and their life cycle is around seventeen billion years. The most well-known example is our own Sun, which emits many different colors that combine to make its light look white to us.

VISIBLE IN THE NIGHT SKY · TAU CETI

K-TYPE STARS (ORANGE DWARFS)

These are orange stars, and at 3,700 to 5,200 K, they're cooler than our Sun. Scientists often focus on K-type stars in the search for extra-terrestrial life because of their long lives—they can live for 30 billion years, which gives plenty of time for life forms to evolve.

VISIBLE IN THE NIGHT SKY · SIRIUS

M-TYPE STARS (RED DWARFS)

Red dwarf stars are incredibly common; they may make up around 75 percent of the stars in the Milky Way. Their temperatures are only about 4,000 K (they're the coolest main-sequence star type), but they can theoretically live for an incredibly long time: trillions of years, much longer than the universe has been around.

UNFORTUNATELY, BECAUSE THEY'RE RELATIVELY DIM, WE CAN'T ACTUALLY SEE ANY RED DWARF STARS FROM EARTH WITH THE NAKED EYE.

ASTERISM
THE BIG DIPPER

CONSTELLATION
URSA MAJOR

CONSTELLATIONS AND ASTERISMS

The IAU, or International Astronomical Union, recognizes eighty-eight official constellations. Some—like Ursa Major and Orion—you might've heard of. Others, you probably haven't. Many won't even be visible from where you live, as the skies in the Northern and Southern Hemispheres are different (northerners will never see the Crux, for example).

But what a lot of people think of as constellations are actually *asterisms*. These are groupings of stars within the sky that form a recognizable pattern, such as the Big Dipper, Little Dipper, and Summer Triangle. Many asterisms are parts of constellations, but they aren't officially recognized as constellations.

That's because constellations have an official purpose: They're regions designated to help people find objects within the night sky. These designations are not actually about naming the most recognizable patterns of stars across the sky; instead, they're chosen to highlight the single most striking pattern in each one of eighty-eight regions of the sky for scientific and observation purposes.

If you're ready to start identifying constellations, then feel free to move on to the next chapter.

Do not look at STARS
as BRIGHT SPOTS only.
Try to take in the
VASTNESS OF THE UNIVERSE.

—Maria Mitchell, *astronomer (1818–1889)*

III.

SEVENTEEN CONSTELLATIONS
TO LOOK FOR

Y ou don't need direction to use the night sky to stargaze for mindfulness. You can just walk outside, look up, and focus on what you can see—or if it's a cloudy night, you can even focus on what's obscuring the things you know are there somewhere. But if you'd like more direction, this chapter can help.

There are eighty-eight official constellations recognized by the IAU. Around thirty are visible from the Northern Hemisphere at any given time of the year and of night (stars do rise and set, just like the Sun does!), though it depends on where you're located.

You should be able to see, at minimum, four constellations of the zodiac plus five circumpolar constellations (though not necessarily all at once, depending on your location).

In this chapter, we'll cover seventeen constellations that are easy to find in the Northern Hemisphere and can be seen with the unaided eye. We'll start with the always-visible circumpolar constellations, which appear to move counterclockwise around a fixed spot in the sky over the course of a year. They rotate around our northern celestial pole, Polaris—also called the North Star. We'll then move on to seasonal constellations, so no matter the time of year or whether you're out in the late-evening or predawn hours, you'll always have something to see.

CIRCUMPOLAR CONSTELLATIONS

There are quite a few circumpolar constellations, but five are visible from almost anywhere in the Northern Hemisphere. These are Ursa Major, Ursa Minor, Draco, Cassiopeia, and Cepheus.

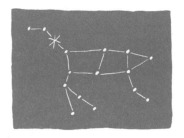

URSA MAJOR

▶ **VISIBLE:** *Year-round but highest in the sky in spring and summer evenings*

Ursa Major is the second largest constellation visible from the Northern Hemisphere, after Virgo (page 122). It's one of the most famous constellations, mainly because the asterism known as the Big Dipper is contained within it.

The Big Dipper is one of the most recognizable and visible objects in the night sky (besides the moon, of course), which means you can use it to find the North Star, Polaris, and from there locate other circumpolar constellations. It looks, basically, like a huge ladle.

In Greek mythology, Ursa Major is associated with the nymph Callisto, who became a bear, was killed, and then was placed among the stars. But various cultures around the world have found meaning in these stars for thousands of years. In the Hindu tradition, the seven stars of the Big Dipper are known as the Saptarishi, or seven sages.

URSA MINOR

▶ **VISIBLE:** *Year-round across the Northern Hemisphere*

U rsa Minor might be dimmer than Ursa Major, but it's relatively easy to locate using the Big Dipper as a reference point. Along with Ursa Major, Ursa Minor is one of forty-eight constellations cataloged by Greek astronomer Ptolemy.

Locate the two easternmost stars in the Big Dipper asterism—the two stars that make up the top and bottom points of the ladle, on the opposite side from the handle. In your mind, draw a line between those two stars, called Dubhe and Merak, and move your gaze northward along that line. You should hit a bright star at the end of the Little Dipper asterism, which makes up part of Ursa Minor.

That bright star is Polaris, the North Star. In the Northern Hemisphere's night sky, the always-visible circumpolar constellations rotate around this star, which always points north. That's why Polaris (located about 434 light years away) has been crucial throughout the centuries as a focal point for celestial navigation, because it doesn't move in our sky.

However, Polaris will not be a polestar forever. As the Earth rotates on its own axis every 24 hours, it also "wobbles." That means it's making a much slower, much smaller circle with its poles. It takes twenty-six thousand years to complete one rotation. Because of this wobble, in two thousand years, Errai, within the constellation Cepheus (page 90), will become the new polestar.

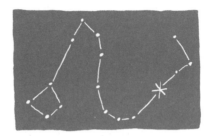

DRACO

▶ **VISIBLE:** *Highest in the sky from April to June*

D raco (the dragon) is the eighth-largest constellation in the sky and is made up of fourteen stars, the brightest of which is called Thuban. However, because none of its individual stars is overly bright, it's not as well known as the Ursas Major and Minor.

To find Draco, locate the Big Dipper and Polaris. Halfway between the North Star and the bowl of the Big Dipper, you'll find the tail of the great dragon. Arabic astronomy conceives of this constellation not as a dragon, but as part of a larger grouping of stars that depicts a group of hyenas attacking a baby camel that is protected by adult camels.

Ancient Egyptians oriented the Great Pyramid of Giza to align with Thuban, which was the North Star around five thousand years ago when it was built. The star is located about 270 light years away and has the dubious distinction of being one of the faintest polestars in history.

Located within the constellation of Draco is a marvel that that you need a telescope to view—Abell 2218. This is a galaxy cluster about 2 billion light years away. Scientists used it as a gravitational lens to find a galaxy about 13 billion light years away, one of the most distant objects ever seen. (Gravitational lensing is a feature of relativity that occurs when a distribution of matter, such as a cluster of galaxies, magnifies an even more distant object along the same path.)

CASSIOPEIA

▶ **VISIBLE:** *Easiest to see in fall and winter*

I t's pretty easy to find Cassiopeia because it's such a bright constellation, visible even during a full moon. An asterism within it, containing the constellation's five brightest stars, forms a prominent "W" within the night sky. Locate the Big Dipper, then draw a line in the night sky to Polaris. Keep moving along that line and you'll find the edges of Cassiopeia.

Traditional Greek origins of Cassiopeia associate this constellation with its neighbor, Cepheus (we'll get to that one next).

Cassiopeia was an Ethiopian queen and the mother of Andromeda. She was boastful about her own beauty, and Poseidon sought to punish her as a result. Cassiopeia and her husband, King Cepheus, tried to sacrifice their daughter Andromeda to appease the sea god, but she was rescued by Perseus. Poseidon then placed the husband and wife in the heavens as a punishment.

Other cultures around the world also have stories about the prominent "W" asterism. In Cree tradition, the constellation is an elk skin stretched and drying on wooden stakes—the stakes are, of course, the stars. Among the Navajo, it is called Náhookòs Bi'áád and is considered a female companion to the Big Dipper.

Cassiopeia contains some pretty amazing astronomical phenomena, including Rho Cassiopeiae, one of just a handful of known yellow hypergiant stars. The supernova remnant Cassiopeia A, not visible to the unaided eye, is one of the brightest known sources of radio waves outside our solar system.

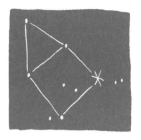

CEPHEUS

▶ **VISIBLE:** *Year-round generally, but most prominent in August through November*

Cepheus is another faint constellation. It's easiest to identify through its asterism that looks like a stick drawing of a house; the triangular "roof" always points towards Polaris. To find it, first locate its partner constellation, Cassiopeia. The two halves of Cassiopeia's "W" aren't symmetrical. If you find the narrower, deeper half and trace a line from its outer end star, called Caph, and continue the line of the "V" outward away from Cassiopeia, you'll stumble upon the bottom of Cepheus's house asterism.

In the ancient Greek tradition, both Cepheus and Cassiopeia are part of the Perseus group of constellations, along with Andromeda, their daughter. In ancient Chinese astronomy, you can find the stars of Cepheus in two different regions of the sky: the Purple Forbidden enclosure (one of the three enclosures centered on the celestial pole) and the Black Tortoise of the North symbol.

The brightest star in Cepheus is Alpha Cephei, or Alderamin, a fast-spinning white star about 49 light years away. It's believed to be at the end of its main-sequence life and is in the process of becoming a supergiant star.

Cepheus is known for playing host to the first example of a Cepheid variable star, Delta Cephei. Cepheid variables are stars that pulse in size and temperature. They operate on a predictable schedule, and the length of time between pulses is directly tied to their brightness. This makes it simple to accurately calculate the distance to Cepheid variables; Delta Cephei is 891 light years away.

SUMMER CONSTELLATIONS

Summer constellations are brightest in June, July, and August in the Northern Hemisphere. Since the night starts late and doesn't last as long in the summer, you have to work a little harder to see Cygnus, Lyra, Scorpius, and Sagittarius, but they're worth the effort!

CYGNUS

▶ **VISIBLE:** *June through December*

ygnus, meaning swan in Latinized Greek, is one of the easiest constellations to find in the summer sky. It's the shape of a cross—sometimes it's called the Northern Cross asterism. But there's another asterism that makes it even easier to find Cygnus, called the Summer Triangle, which contains stars from three different constellations. The Summer Triangle is easy to spot for two reasons. First, it consists of three of the brightest stars in the night sky: Deneb, Vega, and Altair. Second, there are no other exceptionally bright stars in their vicinity. Just look straight up and find the prominent triangle in the night sky. It's visible for most of the night throughout the summer.

Look for the brightest star in the Summer Triangle—Vega. Draw a line westward to the other star in the asterism. This is Deneb, which forms the tail of the swan, Cygnus. Deneb is located about 1,400 light years away and is the North Star for Mars.

Cygnus may have been known as Tuulalupe, or "pigeon roost," by the Tongans, who used it for navigation. If you're surprised by the translation, remember that from these Pacific islands in the Southern Hemisphere, the Tongans would have seen Cygnus upright, like a bird perch.

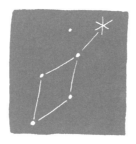

LYRA

▶ **VISIBLE:** *June through October*

L yra is a small constellation, supposedly shaped like the lyre of Orpheus from Greek mythology. To our eyes, much of it looks like a parallelogram.

If you've located Cygnus, it's easy to find the constellation Lyra. Go back to the Summer Triangle and find the brightest star, Vega, again. Vega is one corner of the small four-sided shape that makes it easy to identify the constellation Lyra.

While Lyra doesn't have a lot of significance throughout history and across cultures, the star Vega certainly does. In Sanskrit, Vega is known as Abhijit, and it's considered an auspicious star in Hindu astrology dating back to the epic *The Mahabharata*.

Vega is the fifth-brightest star in the night sky and the second-brightest star visible in the Northern Hemisphere. It's located about 25 light years away, and it may have at least one exoplanet (a planet from outside our solar system) in its orbit. If you've seen or read Carl Sagan's *Contact*, you may be familiar with Vega—it's where the signal Ellie Arroway discovers originates.

Vega is bluish white, which you can see even with the unaided eye, and it's visible even in light-polluted areas. Generally the stars of the Summer Triangle are the first ones visible after the Sun sets. (The third star in the Summer Triangle is Altair, in the constellation Aquila, or the Eagle, which we won't be discussing in depth in this book.)

SCORPIUS

▶ **VISIBLE:** *The brightest constellation in the July night sky, but visible through mid-September*

Scorpius, an astrological constellation, is one of the oldest constellations in recorded history, with documentation going back over five thousand years to the ancient Sumerians—way before the ancient Greeks. It's traditionally a Southern Hemisphere constellation, but we can spot it in the Northern Hemisphere during the summers.

To find Scorpius, orient yourself southward and look low in the sky in the evening, around 9 p.m. Look for a bright, red star along the horizon. That's Antares, the heart of the scorpion. Depending on your location and observation time, you'll also see a hook-shaped formation of stars below that.

To many, Scorpius doesn't look much like a critter. In Hawaiian tradition, Scorpius is Maui's fishhook, made popular by the Disney movie *Moana*. The demigod Maui used that hook to pull the Hawaiian islands up from the depths of the sea.

Scorpius is located right next to the great arm of the Milky Way, and there are many astronomical wonders located within the constellation. Messier 7, for instance, is an open star cluster (a loosely bound group of tens or hundreds of stars) visible to the unaided eye on a dark night—follow the hook, or the tail of the scorpion, to its end and you'll see M7 as a bright, fuzzy spot in the night sky.

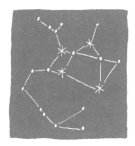

SAGITTARIUS

▶ **VISIBLE:** *June through early September, most visible in August*

Sagittarius is another zodiac constellation located in the southern summer sky. Like Scorpius, it's mostly a Southern Hemisphere constellation, but it's high in our skies during summer nights. If you're observing the skies from a dark place, you'll see that the constellation lies within the ghostly band of the Milky Way.

Sagittarius is remarkable for another reason: It marks the direction of the center of the galaxy. About 26,000 light years away lurks a quiet supermassive black hole called Sagittarius A* (yes, you have to pronounce the "star"). It's in the western part of Sagittarius. Despite the fact that it has a luminous *accretion disk* (that is, a rotating disk of accumulating matter) surrounding it, we can't actually see it with the unaided eye because it's shrouded by dust.

To find Sagittarius, find the Summer Triangle. Draw a line from Deneb, in Cygnus, through Altair, and keep going straight. You'll hit Sagittarius near the horizon. Look for a teapot-shaped asterism within the constellation, which is formed by Sagittarius's brightest stars.

We can trace the recorded history of Sagittarius back to Sumerian times, possibly as far back as 4500 BCE. The Sumerians associated the constellation with their god Nergal, a winged horse with one human head and one big cat head, as well as a scorpion-style stinger instead of a tail.

WE ARE ALL STARDUST

When you're feeling like you don't matter
or you're burned out, try this meditation.

It's easy to feel lost in a busy, moving world.
When you do, remember that we are all made of
stardust. Most elements heavier than hydrogen,
including those that make up our bodies,
originated in the stars.

Think of a star, burning hot, fusing hydrogen
at its core. Meditate on the fire within that
star—much like the fire that burns inside you.
If you're feeling empty, remember that stars
keep burning after the hydrogen inside them
is gone—the fusion just moves on to helium.
Focus on that star, and think about the fuel
you use. Is it food or something to nourish the
soul? Have you been taking care of yourself?

AUTUMN CONSTELLATIONS

These next constellations—Perseus, Andromeda, and Pegasus—are best viewed in September, October, or November. As the temperatures cool off, don't forget to bring a cozy blanket and a hot thermos to ensure your stargazing experience is comfortable.

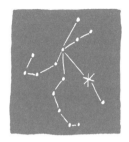

PERSEUS

▶ **VISIBLE:** *August through March*

Perseus follows Cassiopeia through autumn evenings in the Northern Hemisphere. While the constellation can be a challenge to find on its own, if you locate Cassiopeia, it's a simple line to Perseus. Look into the sky and find the "W" of Cassiopeia. If it's shaped like an "M," look to the southeast in the sky. If it's shaped like a "W," look to the southwest. When you see a yellow star (this is called Mirfak, which is at the center of Perseus) and a blue-white star (called Algol), you've found the Perseus constellation.

This constellation is said to resemble the Greek hero Perseus holding aloft his sword and the snake-haired head of Medusa, who he slayed. While the story of Perseus is a well-known Greek myth, the star Algol has significance around the world. Because it's a *trinary star system* (that is, three stars that orbit one another), there are regular eclipses, which change the brightness of the star, as seen from the Earth. As a result, Algol is associated with bad omens throughout history. The Ancient Egyptians were the first to observe Algol's variability and associated it with "ghoulish habits."

You may have gazed straight at Perseus in the past if you've ever gone outside to watch the Perseid meteor shower. The Perseids occur every year in July and August, peaking around August 10. They appear across the sky but seem to originate within Perseus. The Perseids are a favorite of stargazers because it's a steady meteor shower with many colorful trails, and it rarely disappoints. Predawn is the best time to see it.

ANDROMEDA

▶ **VISIBLE:** *June through February, but easiest to see from September on*

Andromeda is among the largest of Ptolemy's original list of forty-eight constellations. It consists of sixteen stars in our night sky and is easy to find thanks to neighboring Cassiopeia. Find the "W" of Cassiopeia, then follow the two outer lines as they slope toward each other. Keep following those imaginary lines through the sky as if they're going to meet, and you'll arrive at Andromeda. The shape is supposed to be of a woman, but early Arabic astronomers saw a fish in these stars.

The Andromeda constellation is home to three bright stars—Alpheratz, Mirach, and Almach—but the true treasure of this small patch of the night sky is something else entirely: the Andromeda galaxy, also known as M31. Remember that Andromeda is 2.5 billion light years away, and it's the farthest object visible with the unaided eye in our night sky. Just because M31 is technically visible to the naked eye doesn't make it easy to spot, though. Make sure it's a dark night; you may not be able to find the galaxy at all if you're stargazing from a city. If you're ready to look, locate the Andromeda constellation. If you have a sense of the shape of the constellation, find her left hip. That's the star Mirach. If it all just looks like a bunch of stars to you, then find Cassiopeia again. The deeper of the two Vs in that constellation points roughly at Mirach, which is located about 200 light years away.

Once you've found the bright star Mirach, follow Andromeda's leg down to another star (Mu Andromedae), then keep traveling in a line out from that second star. You should be able to just make out a faint smudge of light in the sky. It may actually be easier to see if you don't look directly at it. This is the Andromeda galaxy. If you're still struggling to spot it, flip to page 109 and try again using the Great Square of Pegasus.

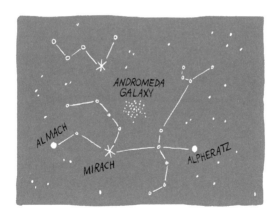

PEGASUS

▶ **VISIBLE:** *August through December, but best in September and October*

The constellation Pegasus, so-named for the great winged horse on which Perseus flew to rescue Andromeda from the sea monster, is in the same area of the sky as the constellations Perseus and Andromeda. It's notable for the giant square asterism that makes up the horse's body (only the top half of the horse—its body, head, and two front legs—makes up the constellation). To locate it, find Polaris, and then draw a line to the outer star in Cassiopeia's deeper

V, Caph. Keep going and you'll hit the Great Square of Pegasus.

The four stars in the Great Square are Alpheratz, Scheat, Markab, and Algenib. You can use them to find the Andromeda galaxy, or M31. Locate Alpheratz, which is the star closest to the Andromeda constellation (in fact, Pegasus shares it with Andromeda). Hop from Alpheratz to Mirach, then Mu Andromedae, and from there you can find M31.

The Anishinabe of present-day Canada see Pegasus not as a winged horse but as a moose. Just turn the constellation around—the body is still made of the Great Square, but the horse's legs become the moose's antlers, and there's even a little fur under the chin.

WINTER CONSTELLATIONS

Constellations that are easiest to spot in the winter months (i.e. December—February) include Orion, Taurus, and Gemini. Long winter nights mean more viewing time, and winter skies can often be crystal clear. Even if it's cold, try to make the most of these months!

ORION

▶ **VISIBLE:** *August to April, but most visible in the winter and early spring*

O rion is the most prominent and easy-to-spot winter constellation, thanks to the line of three stars that makes up the hunter's belt. To find it, orient yourself southwestward and gaze up. You should easily be able to make out the asterism of three bright stars in a line. From there, see if you can spot the hourglass shape of the hunter's head, body and legs above and below the belt. Many cultures see the three stars not as a belt but as animals—the Sotho of southern Africa see them as three pigs in the sky.

The constellation contains some of the brightest stars in our night sky. Rigel is a blue-white star that makes up the hunter's right leg, while Betelgeuse is a red supergiant that is the hunter's left shoulder. Betelgeuse is well known for many reasons (it's one of the top ten brightest stars in our night sky), but it made recent news because of an inexplicable dimming. At first, scientists thought it was about to go supernova, but it returned to its original brightness level. Now, researchers know that the star itself belched a cloud of dust that dimmed Betelgeuse from our perspective.

The constellation is also home to the Orion Molecular Cloud Complex, which is the nearest star-forming region to our own solar system (around 1,400 light years from us). It contains many famous *nebulae* (areas of gas and dust) and star clusters. Thanks to this, Orion is home to many remarkable deep space objects; while binoculars or a small telescope would grant you spectacular views, you can still do some spotting with the unaided eye.

One such sighting is the Orion Nebula, one of the brightest nebulae in our night sky. To find it, locate the hunter's belt, then move your gaze downward to the sword hanging from it. About halfway down the sword, you'll see a fuzzy object that might be easier to spot when you're not looking directly at it. That's the Orion Nebula, or M42.

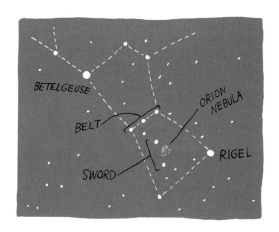

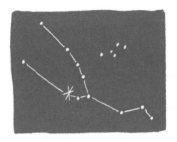

TAURUS

▶ **VISIBLE:** *October to March, but best viewed in October and November*

Taurus is another zodiac constellation, and it's unsurprising that it's been interpreted as a bull across cultures and history. When you look at this pattern of stars, it's relatively easy to make out the legs, body, head, and horns. Ancient Egyptians interpreted the constellation as representing Apis, the bull, an incarnation of Osiris.

To find the bull, locate the easy-to-spot Orion and find his belt. Follow an imaginary line through the sky northward, and you'll hit the "face" of Taurus the bull. The star Aldebaran is prominent here; its reddish-orange hue makes it look as though it's the shining eye of the bull. The star's name is derived from Arabic and means "the follower," because it appears to follow the two prominent star clusters located in Taurus. (If you're a *Star Trek* fan, you're probably familiar with Aldebaran whiskey.)

The first cluster is the Hyades cluster, and along with Aldebaran, it makes up the head of the bull. It's Earth's nearest open star cluster (a group of stars born around the same time from gas and dust), just 150 light years away. The main grouping of stars in the cluster are about 15 light years across. While Hyades is remarkable in and of itself, it pales in comparison to the other star cluster located in Taurus.

The Pleiades, or Seven Sisters, appear throughout the stories of ancient cultures as a hallmark for the changing of the seasons. To find this open star cluster, which makes up the tail of the bull, locate Orion's belt, then Aldebaran, and keep going on that imaginary line. You'll arrive at the Pleiades. While the cluster has around one thousand stars, you can see about fourteen with the unaided eye in good viewing conditions.

NEBRA SKY DISC
C. 1800-1600 BCE

GEMINI

► **VISIBLE:** *September to May, but best viewed January through March*

The zodiac constellation Gemini is most notable for yellowish Castor and bluish-white Pollux, the two bright stars that form the heads of the twins. These stars have been grouped together throughout history. Ancient Hawaiians described the twin stars of Nanamua and Nanahope as one of their twenty-six constellations, which seem to align with Castor and Pollux.

To find Gemini, locate Orion. Draw a line from Rigel through Betelgeuse and keep moving. When you hit two bright stars close together, you'll know you've found the constellation Gemini.

Gemini is also home to the Geminids meteor shower, which occurs in late November and December but usually peaks in mid-December. When there's no moon, observers can view up to 120 meteors per hour in the predawn hours. The Geminids are unique in that, unlike every other meteor shower, they're caused by an asteroid, 3200 Phaethon, and not a comet.

Comets are made up of ice, dust, and rocks, while asteroids are just rocks (and sometimes metals). That's why comets have tails; tails are actually dust and part of the ice melting off. Meteor showers occur when the Earth passes through this debris, which asteroids usually don't have. So why does 3200 Phaethon cause a meteor shower? Scientists aren't quite sure, but one theory is that it's a dead former comet and the Geminids are produced by the debris it used to leave in its wake.

SPRING CONSTELLATIONS

From March through May,
look out for Boötes and Virgo
in the Northern Hemisphere,
two of the biggest constellations
in the night sky.

BOÖTES

▶ **VISIBLE:** *Highest in the sky in June, but generally visible from January through September*

You may not have heard of Boötes, but it's one of the largest constellations in the night sky. Unlike Scorpius and Sagittarius, it's visible for most of the year from the Northern Hemisphere. It's pretty easy to spot, thanks to the kite-shaped asterism contained within the constellation and the star Arcturus. Locate the Big Dipper. Draw a curved line southwest from the end of the handle, and you'll find Arcturus, which is the bottom of the kite.

Arcturus is bright in our sky because it's relatively close to us—just 36.7 light years away. Its orange color is due to the fact that it's in the late stages of its life. Unlike our Sun, which is still on the main sequence, Arcturus has fused all the hydrogen in its core and is now a red giant. Eventually, it will likely become a white dwarf.

Hindus call this star Swathi (or Swati, depending on the region you're from). It's the brightest star visible from the Northern Hemisphere, and the fourth-brightest star visible from Earth after Sirius, Canopus, and our nearest neighbor, Alpha Centauri.

If you're not sure how to bring up Boötes in a conversation with friends, the pronunciation is simpler than it seems. The umlaut just means that the *o's* should be pronounced individually—think "bo-oh-tees."

SPRING CONSTELLATIONS

VIRGO

▶ **VISIBLE:** *March to July, and highest in the sky on May evenings*

Virgo, the maiden, is another zodiac constellation that lies along the ecliptic. It's the second largest constellation behind Hydra, which is also visible during the spring from the Northern Hemisphere. However, Hydra contains no bright, notable stars (and can therefore be a bit difficult to find).

You can find the constellation Virgo using the Big Dipper and Arcturus, in Boötes. Follow the Big Dipper's handle to Arcturus, and then keep on going along this curved line. The next bright object you arrive at is Spica, a blue-white star that's part of a multi-star system. (Right now, scientists think this system is binary, but it's possible there are more stars we haven't yet detected.) Spica forms part of the maiden's torso, which has wings.

You can't see it with the unaided eye, but within Virgo is the Virgo cluster, a group of about two thousand galaxies located around 65 million light years away. It's the closest group of galaxies to our own, the Local Group (of which the Milky Way is a member). The Virgo cluster and Local Group together, along with around fifty other smaller groups of galaxies, make up the Local Supercluster, which has a diameter of about 100 million light years.

Virgo is traditionally associated with spring, the Greek myth of Demeter and Persephone, and the goddess of justice, Dike. In Zulu tradition, Spica is known as iNqonqoli, or the Wildebeest star. Its rise to prominence in the spring signals the beginning of wildebeest season.

THERE ARE AS MANY STARS AS GRAINS OF SAND

This is a great meditation for when you're feeling overwhelmed.

It's hard to conceive of how many stars there are. According to Carl Sagan, there are as many stars in the sky as there are grains of sand on Earth. How can our minds even comprehend that scale?

We can't, and we don't need to try. Instead, use the idea of the universe's vastness to center yourself. Picture yourself, wherever you are right now. Zoom out—what town or city are you in? What state, province, or region are you in? Repeat this until you're focusing on the planet Earth as a whole.

And then go even farther.

Picture our planet, a blue-green gem suspended in the empty space around us. We're part of a solar system, which is part of a larger galaxy. That galaxy is part of a Local Group, which is a member of a supercluster of galaxies. Keep zooming out until you can't anymore, and then bring your focus back to you. The universe is vast, incomprehensible. And you are important in it.

Aveni, Anthony. "Star Stories: Constellations and People." Yale University Press, 2019.

Beall, Abigail. "The Art of Urban Astronomy: A Guide to Stargazing Wherever You Are." Trapeze, 2021.

Dickinson, Terence, and Alan Dyer. "The Backyard Astronomer's Guide." 4th ed. Firefly Books, 2021.

Holbrook, Jarita C., Johnson O. Urama, and R. Thebe Medupe, eds. "African Cultural Astronomy: Current Archaeoastronomy and Ethnoastronomy Research in Africa." Springer Science+Business Media, 2008.

International Dark-Sky Association, The. (Website.) Accessed August 5, 2022. https://www.darksky.org/

Johnson, Sarah Stewart. "The Sirens of Mars: Searching for Life on Another World." Crown Publishing, 2020.

Levesque, Emily. "The Last Stargazers: The Enduring Story of Astronomy's Vanishing Explorers." Sourcebooks, 2020.

Marchant, Jo. "The Human Cosmos: Civilization and the Stars." Dutton, 2020.

Prescod-Weinstein, Chanda. "The Disordered Cosmos: A Journey into Dark Matter, Spacetime, and Dreams Deferred." Bold Type Books, 2021.

Society of Māori Astronomy Research and Traditions. "Resources." Accessed August 5, 2022. https://www.maoriastronomy.co.nz/resources

SWAPNA KRISHNA is a journalist specializing in space, science, technology, and science fiction. She is the host of *Far Out* on PBS and a regular contributor to *New Scientist*, *Wired*, NPR, *StarTrek.com*, and *StarWars.com*. She is the coeditor of *Sword Stone Table*, an anthology of inclusive retellings of King Arthur and the Knights of the Round Table lore. Swapna lives in Philadelphia, PA.

SEE MORE
BOOKS IN
THE SERIES

THE POCKET NATURE SERIES offers meditative and insightful guides to reconnecting with the natural world through mindful practices.

WWW.CHRONICLEBOOKS.COM/POCKETNATURE